Happy

from DESPICABLE ME 2

Words and Music by Pharrell Williams

Arranged by Sylvia Woods
for solo harp and harp duet

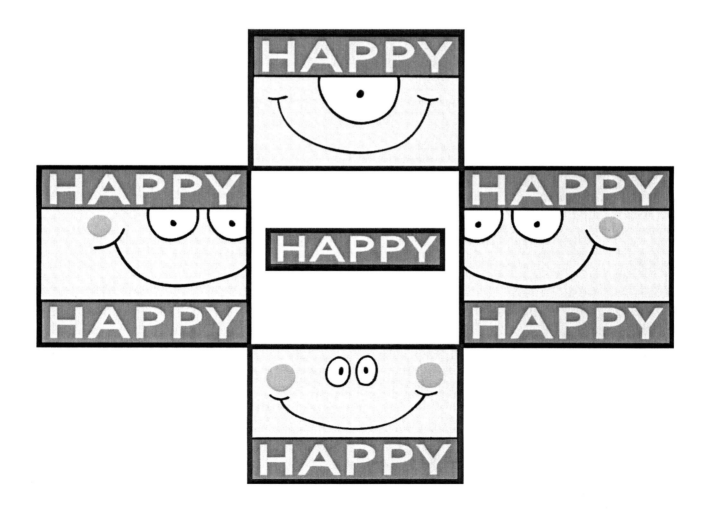

Performance Notes

CHORDS: All of the chords in this music should be played flat, which means you do not roll or arpeggiate them. You play all of the notes of the chord at the same time.

SHARPING LEVERS: If you play a lever harp, be sure to set your sharping levers as indicated before you begin. Lever changes are indicated with diamond notes and also with octave wording between the treble and bass staves. Pedal changes for pedal harps are printed below the bass staff.

FINGERINGS: You are welcome to change any fingerings to suit your own preferences. There are several ways to finger certain passages, particularly when the same note is repeated. If you decide to change a fingering, be sure to write it in the music and play it the same way each time. Using consistent fingering will help you to learn and remember the music.

MEASURE NUMBERS: The measures for the solo and duet parts are not always on the same page or the same staff. For ensemble practice purposes, use the measure numbers at the beginning of each stave.

CODAS: If you are not familiar with "D.S. al Coda," here's what it means. At the end of measure 49 at the D.S. al Coda go back to the 𝄋 at measure 18. Play from there through measure 33 again, then skip ahead to the Coda (ending) at measure 50.

Muffles

Muffles are a standard part of pedal harp technique. However, many lever harp players are not familiar with them. There are two types of muffles used in this piece. The muffles are optional, but including them will make the music cleaner, crisper, and *jazzier*. In each instance, you do not play the notes that are part of the symbol, they just show you which strings need to be muffled. Here's what the muffle symbols mean.

 Place your left hand flat against the strings between the notes indicated. In this piece, you will be muffling the octave below middle C to quiet the notes you played in the previous measure.

This symbol means to lightly replace your fingers on the individual strings you just played to muffle them. This gives a staccato effect.

Harp Solo

The harp solo is arranged for advanced beginner harp players. There are several sharping lever changes required, and you need to have levers on F, C, G, and D strings. The harp range needed is 24 strings from B up to D. If you have a 26-string harp with C as the bottom note, you can play this solo if you tune the bottom C string down to a B.

If the chords in the introduction are too hard for you, you can play this instead. If you use this option, you won't need to set the G# lever before you begin, and you can delete the middle G lever change in measure 14.

 You can also turn the 6-note chords in measures 17 and 54 into easier 4-note chords by leaving out the F in the right hand and the higher B in the left.

Harp Duet

Both parts of the duet can be played by advanced beginner harpists. Part 1 is the easier part, and could be played by some beginning students as well. It requires no sharping levers except for the F#s in the key signature. It can be played on a 26-string harp and requires 19 strings from E up to B.

Part 2 of the duet is a bit more advanced than Part 1. Sharping levers are required on F, C, G, and D strings, and there are two lever changes within the piece. The harp range needed is 24 strings from B up to D. If you have a 26-string harp with C as the bottom note, you can play this part if you tune the bottom C string down to a B.

The harp solo can be played along with both parts of the duet if you have a larger ensemble with more advanced players.

Due to copyright restrictions, each player must purchase their own copy of this music. Thank you for your cooperation.

Lyrics

VERSE 1: It might seem crazy what I'm 'bout to say:
Sunshine, she's here; you can take a break.
I'm a hot air balloon that could go to space
With the air like I don't care, baby, by the way.
Here's why:

CHORUS: Because I'm happy.
Clap along if you feel like a room without a roof.
Because I'm happy.
Clap along if you feel like happiness is the truth.
Because I'm happy.
Clap along if you know what happiness is to you.
Because I'm happy.
Clap along if you feel like that's what you wanna do.

VERSE 2: (not in this arrangement)
Here come bad news, talkin' this and that.
Gimme all you got, no holding back.
Well, I should prob'bly warn you, I'll be just fine.
No offense to you, don't waste your time.
Here's why:

BRIDGE: (Happy!) Bring me down, can't nothing
(Happy!) bring me down;
Your love is too high.
(Happy!) Bring me down, can't nothing
(Happy!) bring me down.
(Let me tell you now.)

Happy
Solo Harp Arrangement
from DESPICABLE ME 2

Lever harp players: set your sharping levers for the key signature, and then set the levers shown above.
Sharping lever changes are indicated with diamond notes and also with octave wording. Pedal changes are written below the bass staff.

Please see page 2 for performance notes and information about the muffles used in this arrangement.

Words and Music by Pharrell Williams

Moderately Fast

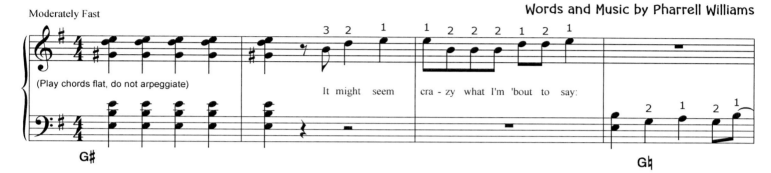

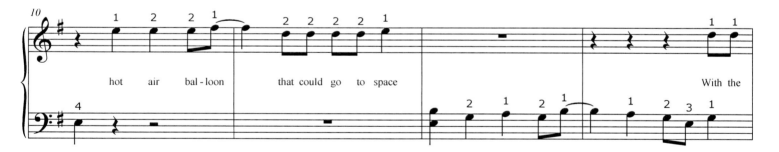

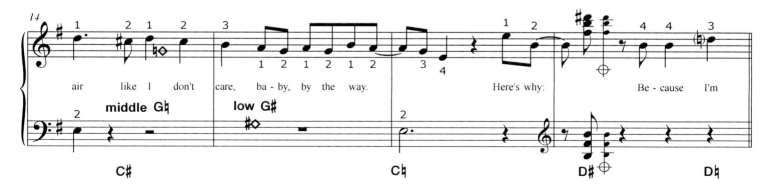

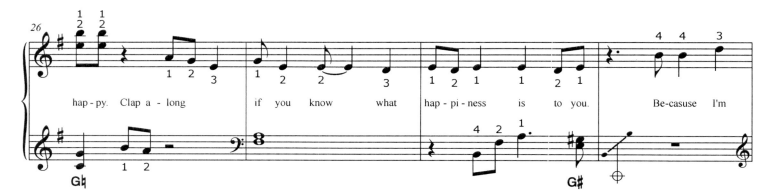

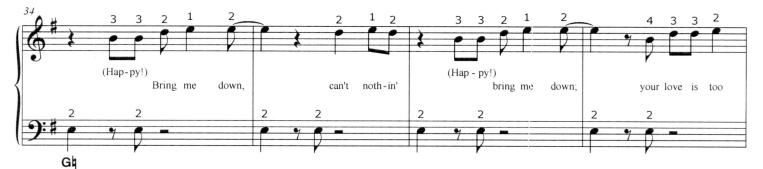

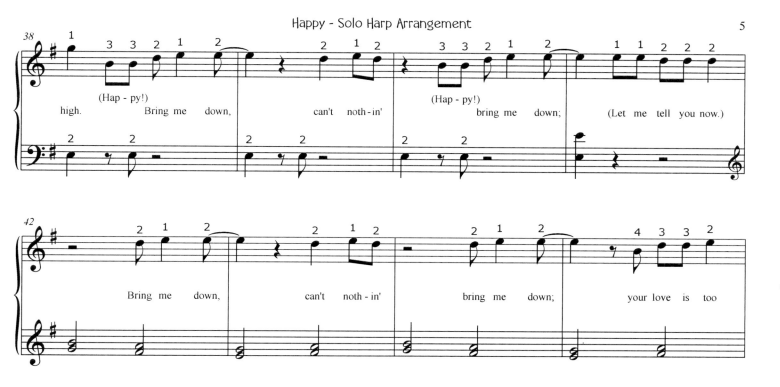

D.S. al Coda

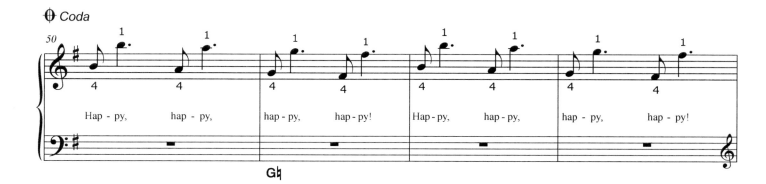

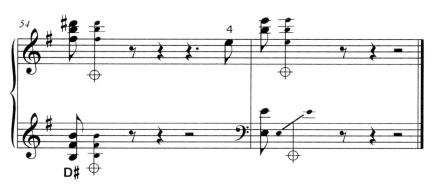

Happy - Harp Duet, Part 1

from DESPICABLE ME 2

Lever harp players: set your F# sharping levers for the key signature. There are no lever changes in this part.

LH means to play with your left hand. RH indicates right hand.
Please see page 2 for performance notes and information about the muffles used in this arrangement.

Words and Music by Pharrell Williams

Moderately Fast

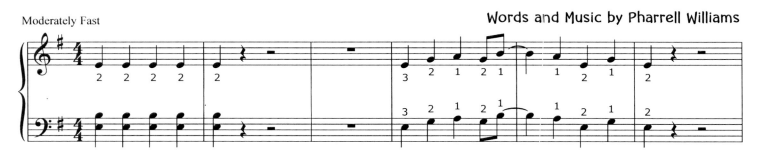

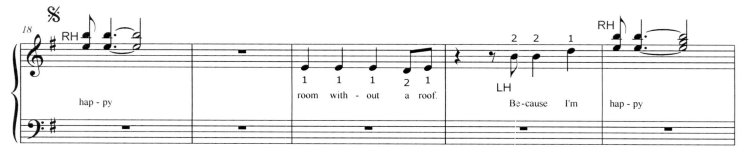

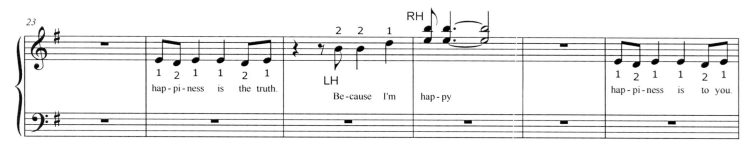

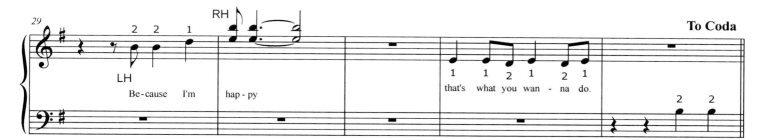

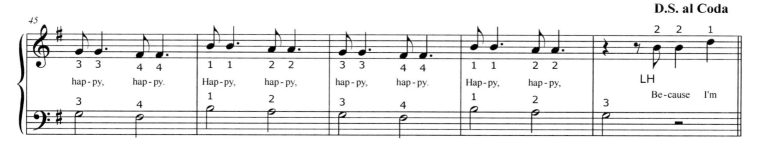

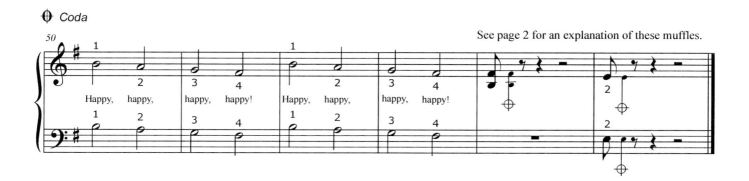

See page 2 for an explanation of these muffles.

Happy - Harp Duet, Part 2
from DESPICABLE ME 2

Lever harp players: set your sharping levers for the key signature, and then set the levers shown above.
Sharping lever changes are indicated with diamond notes and also with octave wording. Pedal changes are written below the bass staff.

Please see page 2 for performance notes and information about the muffles used in this arrangement.

Words and Music by Pharrell Williams

Moderately Fast

It might seem cra-zy what I'm 'bout to say: Sun-shine, she's

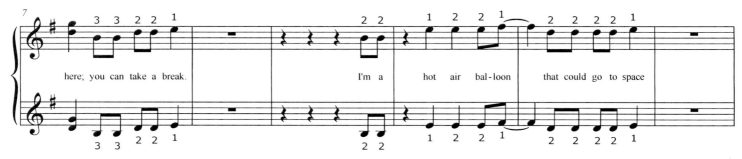

here; you can take a break. I'm a hot air bal-loon that could go to space

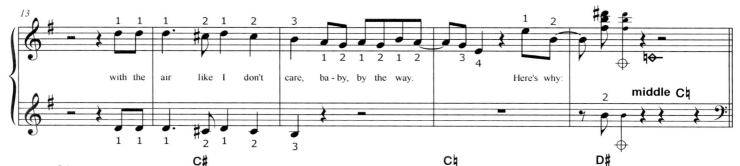

with the air like I don't care, ba-by, by the way. Here's why:

Clap a-long if you feel like a room Clap a-long if you feel like

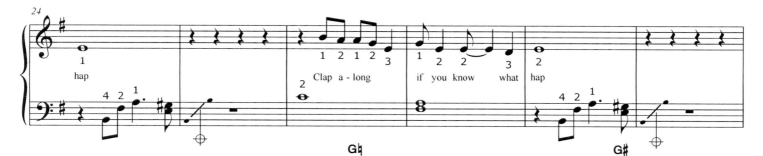

hap Clap a-long if you know what hap

Happy

This sheet music includes Sylvia Woods' solo harp arrangement of Pharrell Williams' hit song "Happy."
An added bonus is an easy duet arrangement for 2 harps.

More Harp Arrangements of Pop Music by Sylvia Woods

All of Me
Beauty and the Beast
Music from Disney-Pixar's Brave
Bring Him Home from Les Misérables
Castle on a Cloud from Les Misérables
A Charlie Brown Christmas
Dead Poets Society
John Denver Love Songs
76 Disney Songs
Fields of Gold
Fireflies
Music from Disney Frozen
Groovy Songs of the 60s
Four Holiday Favorites
House at Pooh Corner

Into the West from The Lord of the Rings
Lennon and McCartney
My Heart Will Go On from Titanic
Over the Rainbow from The Wizard of Oz
River Flows in You
22 Romantic Songs
Safe & Sound
Say Something
Stairway to Heaven
Music from Disney Tangled
A Thousand Years
Andrew Lloyd Webber Music
The Wizard of Oz
Theme from Disney-Pixar's Up

Available from harp music retailers and www.harpcenter.com

ISBN 978-0-936661-51-3

9 780936 661513

U.S. $7.95

8 88680 06480 8

HL00145202

HAL•LEONARD® CORPORATION
960 EAST MARK ST. P.O. BOX 227
WINONA, MINNESOTA 55987

With many thanks to Paul Baker and Denise Grupp-Verbon

Published by Woods Music & Books
P.O. Box 223434, Princeville, HI 96722, U.S.A.
www.harpcenter.com